UNVEILED

Writing prompts that reveal the heart of God

Heidi Kratzke

Unveiled: Writing prompts that reveal the heart of God

Copyright © 2011 Heidi Kratzke
www.unveiledthebook.com

Published and designed by Creative Culture Media
www.creativeculture.cc
Cover and layout by Jonathan Kratzke

For information or bulk orders:
+1 (218) 234-2233 or sales@unveiledthebook.com

International Standard Book Number: 978-0-615-56656-6

Printed in the United States of America.

"But whenever someone turns to the Lord, the veil is taken away. For the Lord is the Spirit, and wherever the Spirit of the Lord is, there is freedom. So all of us who have had that veil removed can see and reflect the glory of the Lord. And the Lord—who is the Spirit—makes us more and more like him as we are changed into his glorious image."

~2 Corinthians 3:16-18

-Contents-

Introduction

Writing is worship. Let me rephrase that. Writing can be worship. Allow me to explain. Picture a room full of people, all writing about some of the most intimate encounters they've had with God. The workshop starts with one teenager who shares his story of how God intervened in the midst of his self-doubt and suicidal thoughts. A woman writes, and then reads, about the comfort she felt in His arms as her children left home for the unknown. A young girl recalls the first time she felt the tangible love of the Lord, tears splashing onto the spiral bound notebook clenched in her hands.

This particular August afternoon started as a writing workshop, and transformed into a time of worship. After pens and paper were distributed, people began writing about their God. He was faithful to show up, as He always is. The task of writing was soon unnoticed as tears and laughter ushered in a time of praise directed to God. A God who is not just faithful to His people, but faithful to each individual. A God who is always speaking truth to us, provided we are willing to listen.

This book is intended to help you on your journey to a more intimate relationship with your Creator God. Whether you choose to work through the writing exercises alone, with a friend, or with a group of writers, one thing is certain: you will encounter God. If there's anything I've learned through my experience of asking questions, writing out prayers, and simply waiting on Him in silence … it's that He is always faithful.

Let this book be more than just pages, more than just creative inspiration. Take the time, all of the time, necessary to let the revelations you write down make their way from the page, past your mind, and into your heart. Be transformed.

Foundational to this book is the understanding that we serve a living God. It is imperative we understand that the same God who spoke to the disciples and His people throughout the pages of the Bible is still alive and still speaking today. Even if you've never heard the voice of God before, I encourage you to take time, quiet yourself, and pray. Ask God to speak to you.

Challenge yourself to listen more and draw closer to the living God as you complete the writing exercises in this book.

Over the past few years, I've noticed an emergence of art and dance within the church. Traveling as a part of Firestarters, an arts-focused ministry, I've witnessed overwhelming creativity from sons and daughters of God. It is possible to write from the spirit and not just the soul. Through writing from the spirit, we can impact people on a spiritual level—prophesying into the future, transforming the now.

As a writer and follower of Jesus, I've found there are very few Christian resources that directly encourage the reader to create, rather than just explain how the creative process evolves. Once a week, I hold a writers group in my home. In planning for this weekly gathering, I've spent many hours developing some of the prompts you'll find in the following pages.

Writers are often represented in a somewhat mystical light. Yet, the true purpose of a writer is simple: to communicate a message in written form. Stripping the craft back to its basics has been critical in my own development as a writer. The verse I frequently return to is Habakkuk 2:2. I like how it reads in the Amplified Bible: *"And the Lord answered me and said, Write the vision and engrave it so plainly upon tablets that everyone who passes may [be able to] read [it easily and quickly] as he hastens by."*

Even if you feel you are not a "writer," there is a place for writing in your life. Do you write notes of encouragement to your friends? Do you journal your thoughts or dreams at night? Do you believe it is important to write down what God is saying in order to share that revelation with others?

These prompts are intended merely as a starting place. Feel free to modify them, skip around to different sections that interest you, or even add your own questions between the lines.

Peel away the excess whenever possible and cut to the root of the message you're working to share. Let's impact the world around us with words.

Near to God

It is possible to have a direct, face-to-face, intimate encounter with Jesus as you write. Your words are worship when offered up in spirit and in truth.

One of the prompts in this section will ask you to write about an encounter you've had with God, first from your perspective and then from His. When utilizing writing as a way to reveal God's love for people, this is one of my favorite prompts to use. It encourages writers to recognize that beyond their own recollection of life, God also has a narrative for every moment we've experienced.

Reading people's responses to this type of prompt reveals much about how they perceive the Lord. Is He an angry God? A kind father? A distant observer? A close friend?

Take these prompts and use them as a starting place in your own conversation with God. Ask questions and then quiet yourself to wait for the answers. In my own life, as with my writing, often it is hardest to remain in that place of silence. With life itself constantly attempting to steal away our seconds, spending time focused on the Lord requires a significant amount of effort.

It helps to find a place to write where you know you won't be disturbed. Sometimes you need to seek out that cozy booth in your neighborhood coffee shop, the overstuffed chair in the corner of your living room, or the park bench tucked away from passing traffic. Seek some solitude and set aside the time required to write.

One thing I've found extremely useful is to pray before I start writing. I ask God to surround me with His presence and to pour out creativity through me. The writing experience is what you make of it. Choose to use it as a time to draw near to God.

If you were taken to the heavenly throne room right now, what one question would you ask God?

Write about a vivid encounter with God from your perspective. Now, switch and write about that exact same encounter, but this time from God's perspective.

Which do you value more: freedom or discipline? Explain your answer.

What is the most common thing
you ask God for in prayer?

Faith the size of a mustard seed can move mountains. Write about a time in your life when you've seen a small amount of faith bring about a big change.

Write about a time when God was your comforter.

What is the cost of following Jesus in your life?

Write about the communion experience without mentioning the word "communion," but instead using the words "common" and "union."

What do you see in the eyes of Jesus?

Each person's gifts and talents are powerful, but we're sorely misguided whenever we start to view each other as the sum of these gifts. Recall a time in your life when you fell into the error of either viewing yourself or someone else as merely the product of various abilities or talents. What caused you to change your mind?

Write a character description of your guardian angel.

Write down a specific prayer of yours that God answered. Did the answer come in the way and time frame you expected it to? Why do you think this is?

Set aside a 30-minute block of time to surround yourself with complete silence. Begin your time of silence with a simple prayer asking God to speak to you. After quieting your thoughts and just listening for 30 minutes, then allow yourself to pick up a pen and paper. What did you hear?

Write down, in detail, a dream you've had that you believe might be from God. Prayerfully ask God for revelation regarding your dream and record anything He shows you.

What is the difference between compassion and love?
Which do you think you display more of in your life?

Using your own life as an example, write about the power of forgiveness.

What is God saying right now?

Jesus turned over the tables of the money changers who had set up shop in the temple. What would Jesus turn over if He walked into your church today? How about if He walked into your home?

What do you do to show God your love for Him?

Write about a specific time when you remember being
in absolute awe of God's natural creation. What did
the environment you found yourself in look like?

Write about a fear you once had that
God helped you overcome.

Compile a list that details what you perceive
as some of the mysteries of God.

What is one of the most powerful ways you've seen God answer the prayer of a family member?

Who is the first person you recall talking to you about having a relationship with Jesus? What was your response?

Faith. Hope. Love. Of these three, which would you like to be more evident in your life right now? What do you plan to do to foster growth in this area?

If the Holy Spirit was a bird, and that bird was a color, what color would it be? Explain your choice.

Describe an encounter you've had with your Creator where one word would have ruined the moment.

What is so amazing about grace?

Think about a time during your childhood when you know God protected you. Write about this memory from the perspective of yourself as a child.

Write a poem titled "A New Man" in which you explain the power of baptism.

Write a journal entry that starts with the following line: "The life of a breaker is formed in the deep."

What is the difference between having faith like a child and being childlike?

What kind of fruit grows on your family tree?

When did you first realize that God loves you?

What does it look like to be a burning man or woman for God?

Encouragement

Sometimes it's as simple as a handwritten letter. A thoughtful, well-timed reminder can instill a renewed sense of hope in its reader. In an age where texts, emails, and phone calls permeate our daily interactions, handwritten communication is quickly becoming a lost art.

In our church, no one has taught me more about this than a woman named Vicki. When I had a minor surgery a few years ago, Vicki showed up the same day with a container of homemade soup and a note card wishing me a quick recovery. When I graduated from college, Vicki sent a letter of congratulations in the mail. When I moved to another country for a few months, her familiar handwriting found me in my foreign surroundings.

Receiving verbal encouragement, from a friend or stranger, can cast rays of light onto even the darkest of days. Those same words, presented in written form, can permeate the cloud cover on any day the recipient rereads what was once written. Love letters, cards from departed loved ones, holiday greetings from familiar souls on the opposite side of the world—these treasures can be found tucked away safely in many households. They serve as a reminder of our value in the world and the impact we have in this life lived alongside people we grow to love.

As I was praying one day about what writing exercise to complete during that night's writers group gathering, I felt strongly compelled to send notes of encouragement to the leaders of our church. Everyone who was attending our group that night was a part of the same local church, where a husband and wife serve as pastors.

Even though I knew simple notes expressing our gratitude for them would be a powerful encouragement to our church leaders, I wanted to use this opportunity to make them feel extra special. I purchased some beautiful, designer stationery and matching envelopes. When the group members arrived that evening, I handed them each two sets of the stationery and explained the activity.

By the end of the night, we had 12 handwritten letters sealed and ready for delivery. After bundling the stacks separately, so they would each receive their own pile of letters, a fellow group member and myself hand-delivered the letters to our pastors' home. Seeing the surprised and grateful expressions on their faces as we delivered the stacks reinforced in my heart the notion that those notes of encouragement had come at the perfect time.

"Therefore encourage one another and build each other up, just as in fact you are doing." (*1 Thessalonians 5:11, NIV*) My prayer is that the results of these prompts have a lasting impact on the people you seek to encourage. Pray and let the Spirit guide you as you work your way through this section of the book.

Write a letter to a friend. Include at least one encouraging scripture.

Compose a letter to your pastor. Include a top ten list of why you appreciate him or her.

Find a note card and write out one of the prayers
the Apostle Paul addressed to a group of people
or person in the Bible. Think of someone in your
life who could benefit from reading that specific
prayer and mail the note card to that individual.

Leave a quick note for your local postal employee thanking him or her for a job well done.

Gather together a group of three or four close friends for a "vision session." One at a time, have people share specific goals they have and things they believe God has shown them they will do in the future. Have the other group members each write down the person's name, followed by the key items the person says. Do this for each group member. After writing down each person's vision for the future, commit to holding one another accountable and praying for the specific items on each person's list.

Write a letter to someone who is serving our country in the United States Armed Forces. Express your appreciation for his or her commitment to protecting our nation.

Select three different people in your life who you don't know very well. Write their names down on a piece of paper with space between each name. Spend five minutes praying for each person and then ask God what you can do to bless that person. After each name, write one thing you commit to doing within the next month to bless that individual.

Think about someone you only met once or twice, but who made a difference in your life. Write about the encounter you had with that person.

Write a poem honoring the life of a parent or grandparent. Make a copy of the poem, frame it, and give it to another family member who had a close connection to the relative you featured in the poem.

Write about the most meaningful gift
anyone has ever given you.

Take time out of your day and dedicate an hour
to pray for someone you know who needs a
breakthrough in his or her life. Ask God to give you
His heart for that individual. After your hour of prayer,
write that individual a note of encouragement.

Write a letter to someone in the ministry who has deeply impacted your life. Let that person know how the seed he or she planted in your life continues to grow.

Encourage yourself! Write a list of 10 things you
are thankful for today. Be as specific as you can.

Think of a specific song that reminds you of someone. Write down the song's lyrics and give them to that person, along with an explanation of why these lyrics remind you of him or her.

Ask a friend to write down a few prayer requests for you to pray about. Commit to praying over this list daily and writing down the answers to prayer when they are received.

Arrange a night where a small group of your close friends gets together and spends the evening praying for each other. Volunteer to write down the prayers that were prayed over each individual. Present each person with his or her own list as a reminder of what was prayed over his or her life.

Write a letter thanking a local government representative for his or her role in improving your community.

Visit a nursing home and volunteer to read poetry to the residents. As soon as you return home, write your own poem about the experience.

Mail a greeting card to someone you know who is sick and let that person know you are praying for his or her recovery.

Write a letter to a child in your life. Let the child know how much he or she means to you.

My personal knowledge on the topic of songwriting is extremely limited. I am, however, blessed to be married to a man who knows a great deal about how to craft a well-timed, captivating song. I recently had the unique opportunity to work alongside my husband, Jonathan, to help him see a song through to completion.

The song started out with a concept I felt God repeatedly highlighting to me. As I continued to receive revelation about the Kingdom of God, both here on earth and in heaven, I wrote out the following three lines:

Your Kingdom come
Here on earth
Here in heaven

These lines became the basis for the song I wanted to write about blurring the line between heaven and earth, about how our worship resonates simultaneously in both realms. The pre-chorus I composed looked like this:

I want to join with the angels
Singing more than just sound
Here in eternity beyond all time

Jonathan worked on developing a melody to complement these lines. Each time he played the song on the piano his fingers landed on the keys in a slightly different way, until, after some time, he announced that the music finally "felt right." From there, we worked together to make the lyrics stronger.

Throughout the revision process, I found myself having to take into consideration new challenges I'd never faced while writing poetry. With a poem, it is important to pay attention to word choices and how the words sound. When writing a song, you not only have to consider word choice and the sounds of the words, but also the "singability" of those words and how they interact with the melody.

By the time the song came to fruition, the pre-chorus lyrics read as follows:

> *I'm going to join with the angels*
> *In the song of the Lord*
> *Here in eternity, beyond all time*
> *In the midst of your glory*
> *Surrounding your throne*
> *Here in eternity, we will sing*

If you're interested in writing songs and don't play an instrument, partner with someone who does. Working with a musician who is familiar with the songwriting process will help you listen for the melodic value of your words. Simple lyrics can be powerful when sung, because the melody of a song carries its own message.

If songwriting is something you've never thought about before, take this opportunity to explore a new way of writing. Seasoned songwriters, let these prompts stretch you creatively and enjoy the process!

Write the lyrics for an original love song directed to Jesus. Make the lyrics as simple as possible.

What instrument moves you the most? Use the sounds created by that instrument as the inspiration for a poem. Focus on selecting words that sound like the musical instrument you chose.

Take the last line of a song you like and use it
as the first line of your own song or poem.

What was the first album you purchased?
Write about the way that album made you
feel then and how you feel about it now.

Compose the lyrics to a song where the chorus compares a lion's mane to flames of fire.

Select an instrumental song and write
your own lyrics to go along with it.

What is your favorite worship song? Why do
you believe it impacts you the way it does?

Use repetition to write the chorus for a song.
Focus on using a repeated word or words to
help build the momentum of the song.

Find two instrumental songs, one in a minor key and one in a major key. First, play the song in the minor key on repeat for 15 minutes. Write about whatever comes to your mind when you hear the song. Next, play the song in the major key on repeat for 15 minutes. Write about whatever you think of during this song. Compare the results of your two writing exercises and note the different themes that arose.

Select a psalm out of the Book of Psalms and read it out loud. Pay close attention to the psalmist's expressions toward God. Inspired by the psalmist's voice in that particular psalm, write your own psalm to God.

Write the lyrics to a song God might have sung after
Adam and Eve ate from the Tree of the Knowledge
of Good and Evil in the Garden of Eden.

What does worship look like? Smell
like? Feel like? Taste like?

Wise Quotes

One of the most profound sentences I ever heard a man utter is the following: "It is a lot easier to put out someone's fire than it is to start a fire in them." This wisdom was shared by my pastor, Pete Thiel, in reference to how we should view the people around us.

What he was saying, essentially, is that we should value and protect the passion for God inside one another. While it is very difficult to help kindle someone's passion for the Lord, it is relatively simple to smother that fire. There's wisdom in choosing patience when dealing with people. There's wisdom in withholding some criticism people deserve in order to help them arrive at the place they should be.

I constantly find myself deep in thought over the words uttered by those around me. Even a few simple words can have the power to challenge people's view of the world and their perception of others.

Our foundational views of life start at an early age, and often mimic the values of our parents or guardians. As they verbally respond to the daily circumstances of life, we pick up on these responses. Often, these words can become our own views without our even realizing it. For example, until I was 18 years old, I was under the impression that tea tasted terrible. Why? My mom doesn't care for the taste of it. It wasn't until my senior year of high school, when I actually tried the beverage, that I discovered how welcome the taste of tea was on my palette.

Even though I ended up adopting a different view than my mother on tea, most of my life experience thus far has validated the verbal assessments I heard from my parents while growing up. Beyond this foundational influence, I am constantly finding inspiration in the wise utterances of others.

When I hear a quote that provokes me to deep contemplation or moves me in a fresh way, I try to write it down in my journal. It's fascinating to look back on the words of others that once spoke to you. Whether the words came from a close friend or a world leader, the following quotes continue to resonate in my own life.

Spend some time pondering these words of wisdom. Pray about the truth conveyed and how you should respond. While knowledge can be simply memorized, wisdom comes from experience. How brightly do you want the following quotes to reflect in your own history? Humbly consider the life-giving, thought-provoking revelations these men and women unearthed as a result of their own life experiences. In the words of poet William Wordsworth, "Wisdom is ofttimes nearer when we stoop than when we soar."

"Justice too long delayed is justice denied."
~Martin Luther King, Jr.

Write about a situation where this
statement would prove true.

"We want, in fact, not so much a father in heaven as a grandfather in heaven—a senile benevolence who, as they say, 'liked to see young people enjoying themselves,' and whose plan for the universe was simply that it might be truly said at the end of each day, 'a good time was had by all.'"
~C.S. Lewis

Write about the error of viewing God as a "grandfather" rather than as our Father.

"It is a lot easier to put out someone's fire than it is to start a fire in them."
~Pete Thiel

What does this quote mean to you? How should it be applied in a ministry setting?

"If you can't feed a hundred people, then feed just one."
~Mother Teresa

Write about an instance in your life where you
witnessed the power of this type of mentality.

*"The only thing you've ever owned is what
you're willing to give away."*
~Michael Tyrrell

Do you agree with this statement? Why or why not?

In his 1953 book, "The Go-Between," author L.P. Hartley's opening line reads: *"The past is a foreign country: they do things differently there."*

What elements of your past seem the most foreign to you?

*"When all you have left to give is worship,
then you are truly broken."*
~Keith Goodson

Have you ever been to that place of brokenness?

"When Jesus performed miracles, he wasn't demonstrating what God can do, but what God can do through a man."
~Bill Johnson

Use this quote as the first sentence in a short story.

"Maybe adventure is simply paying attention to the part of you that wants to be created all over again."
~Linford Detweiler

Write about an adventure you'd like to
set out upon while on this earth.

"You can't walk out on your own story."
~Gregg Goodspeed

Come up with a title that best fits the book that is the story of your life. Explain your choice.

"If we are to better the future we must disturb the present."
~Catherine Booth

Write about someone you know personally whose life is a testament to the truth of this statement.

"If God hasn't answered your prayer yet, here's what you should take that to mean: He hasn't answered your prayer yet."
~Bob Sorge

Write about an unanswered prayer you are leaving in God's hands.

"For every person who has ever lived there will come, at last, a spring he will never see. Glory then in the springs that are yours..."
~Pam Brown

What is there to glory in, in the spring that is yours today?

"You can suffer the pain of change or suffer remaining the way you are."
~Joyce Meyer

Write about a painful transformation that resulted in the refining of your character.

"One reason we are so harried and hurried is that we make yesterday and tomorrow our business, when all that legitimately concerns us is today. If we really have too much to do, there are some items on the agenda which God did not put there. Let us submit the list to Him and ask Him to indicate which items we must delete. There is always time to do the will of God. If we are too busy to do that, we are too busy."
~Elisabeth Elliot

Compile a list of everything you have to do today. Pray over the list and remove the unnecessary items.

"I want you to be concerned about your next door neighbor. Do you know your next door neighbor?"
~**Mother Teresa**

Assemble a small gift basket, complete with a personalized "thinking of you" card. Choose a random day to present your neighbor with the basket.

"It is in vain for man to endeavor to instruct man in those things which the Holy Spirit alone can teach."
~Madame Guyon

Write about something you believe each person has to learn directly from the Holy Spirit.

"Courage is almost a contradiction in terms. It means a strong desire to live, taking the form of a readiness to die."
~G.K. Chesterton

What literary or film character do you believe does an excellent job of displaying true courage? What makes that character courageous?

"The marvelous richness of human experience would lose something of rewarding joy if there were no limitations to overcome. The hilltop hour would not be half so wonderful if there were no dark valleys to traverse."
~Helen Keller

Write a poem where the final line reads:
"joy is cultivated in the valley"

"And this wise man asked me to stop. He said, 'Stop asking God to bless what you're doing. Get involved in what God is doing—because it's already blessed."
~Bono

What is your first reaction to this statement?

*"In Scripture the visitation of an angel is always alarming;
it has to begin by saying 'Fear not.' The Victorian
angel looks as if it were going to say, 'There, there.'"*
~C.S. Lewis

Write about a concept of God you've adopted that
is more influenced by culture than experience.

"It is scarcely possible in most places to get anyone to attend a meeting where the only attraction is God."
~A.W. Tozer

Do you agree with this statement? Why or why not?

"We make our decisions, and then our decisions turn around and make us."
~F.W. Boreham

Write about a facet of your personality that you know was formed by a decision you made in the past.

"Comparison is the thief of joy."
~ **Theodore Roosevelt**

Write about a time in your life when
you discovered this to be true.

A Challenge

Are you ready for a challenge?

There's a time to find satisfaction in your writing just being what it is. To create, and simply to create, is a beautiful thing. However, equally important is the process of refining the original creation. The dedicated writer is always willing to take something that has promise and put in the effort required to bring it to a level of excellence.

One troublesome thing to me is witnessing writers settle for their first draft of anything. Especially when writing about Christian topics, I've noticed a tendency for people to believe that because they created something in collaboration with a creative God, their work needs no revision. A first draft of an inspired piece of writing may be a good start, but it is the editing process that will bring it to a higher level of quality.

When explaining this concept, I enjoy using my husband as an example. He is a talented musician with an incredible, God-given ability. When he writes a song, I often marvel at the beauty that comes forth the very first time the lyrics and melody flow out of him.

That said, I can't imagine him ever settling on the original divine inspiration, devoid of the refining process that follows. Once he completes a song, my husband takes the song and plays it for several musicians, soliciting their feedback. Although he is not obligated to tailor his song to fit all of the suggestions given, he carefully considers the valuable input he receives. The result is a stronger song.

My hope is that some of the writing prompts in this book will inspire you to keep writing beyond the parameters of the given prompts. If you elect to continue writing about a particular topic, seeking the support and critique of fellow writers will be of great value.

Another helpful tool to grow as a writer is to spend time forcing yourself to write in unfamiliar, and sometimes even uncomfortable, ways. If you are a free verse poet, committing yourself to penning your first sonnet is a challenge worth trying. If you've only written in a personal journal, crafting and sharing a prose piece during a writing group session will provide you with a refreshing opportunity to experience the impact your writing can have on the people around you.

These exercises are intended to stretch you as a writer. They each present a writing prompt in a somewhat unusual way. Have fun with these and don't be afraid to try something new. You may be impressed with the results!

Ernest Hemingway was once challenged to write a short story in just six words. His response was: "For sale: baby shoes, never used." Write your own six-word story.

Do you typically write poems that rhyme or those without a set rhyme scheme? Whatever your answer is to this question, challenge yourself to do the opposite.

Write a short prose piece about the color of poverty.

If you could keep only 20 material items,
what would they be? Write a list.

Come up with a poem where the first word of your poem is "white" and the last word is "red."

Write out your testimony in 500 words or fewer.

Create a scenario, either real or fictitious, that reveals the meaning of grace. Have the story itself demonstrate what grace is. Make sure to omit any sentences that might try to tell your readers about grace rather than allowing them to come to the revelation of the meaning of the word on their own.

What is the scent of integrity?

Write a poem with the narrative voice being that of an orphaned child spending his or her first night in the home of an adoptive family.

Sum up your mission as a writer in one sentence.

Write a 26-line poem where the first line begins
with a word that starts with an "a", the second
line a "b", the third line a "c", and so on.

Write about your day from the perspective of your neighbor observing your actions.

Write a brief character description that includes the following sentence: "She flickers like a lighthouse."

Come up with a back-and-forth dialogue where one character tells another character about her relationship with Jesus. Do not use any words to describe Jesus other than "he" or "him."

Create a short story that includes each of the following words: crimson, branch, transform, sight, Tuesday.

Write a poem that starts with the word "caterpillar"
and ends with the word "butterfly."

If you were asked to give the sermon this week at church, what would your topic be? Draft a one-page outline of your sermon.

Write a scene from an unborn baby's perspective. Have the baby narrate the scene from inside the womb of his or her mother.

Draft an essay titled "Why I Write."

_____

_____ _____ _____ _____

_____ _____ _____

_____ _____

_____ _____ _____

_____ _____ _____ _____

Transfer the lines above to a piece of paper. On each "_____" fill in one word to create a short poem.

Start out a journal entry with the following sentence: "I am a tree that bends."

What color is a dream?

Write a scene that describes an eagle's perilous flight through a blizzard, told from the eagle's point of view.

Write either a poem or prose piece, with the central theme being the Father's love. The only restriction is that you cannot use the words "father" or "love" anywhere in your writing.

All in an Image

For one woman it is the piece of art she saw hanging in a gallery. The masterpiece was composed of hundreds of broken mirror sections, arranged to depict the face of Jesus. Coming from a broken place in her own life, the woman was instantly drawn to the art. As she walked closer to the jagged glass composition, the woman caught a reflection of her own face in the artwork. Tears plummeted from her eyes as she let herself be transformed by a newfound revelation of the love of a Man who allowed His body to be broken that she might find wholeness.

Art is a powerful expression of both who the artist is and how that person sees the world. This interactive section of the book will help you draw your writing inspiration from another form of art. A successful artistic collaboration can bring forth new beauty and revelation found only in the joining of two art forms.

The paintings and photographs of other artists are some of my favorite places from which to glean inspiration. Looking at visual art provides me with the opportunity to view the world through the overflow of a fellow artist's vision.

One of my favorite photographs is that of a grizzly old man with deep-set wrinkles and gnarled white hair. You can tell by the look in his eyes that he's taken in much of the world and now sees through it. The black-and-white photo graces the CD cover of my favorite band, Over the Rhine. Beneath the man's photo is the stark album title: *Patience.*

I could look at this man's face for hours. I could write about the adventures I imagine he's had, about the losses he's endured through the years, about the faith in each new day that has propelled him into the present. It's one word printed with one photograph. The beauty is in the mystery. I've found the freedom to make that photo an inspiration of my own. An inspiration based not on the man's life, but on how his image affects my own.

Write a poem titled "Rebirth" about the first
day snow blankets the ground each year.

Pick a person at this baptism and write about
the experience from his perspective.

Old buildings
have their
own stories
to tell. What
is this one's?

Write about an
adventure you
had as a child.

Grab a blank piece of paper. On the left side of the paper draw a quick sketch of a person (it doesn't need to be good, just not a stick figure!) This is your main character. Now fill the right side of the page with a short story featuring this new character you drew.

Write about how this picture illustrates an
attribute of God.

What do this woman's eyes reveal about her life?

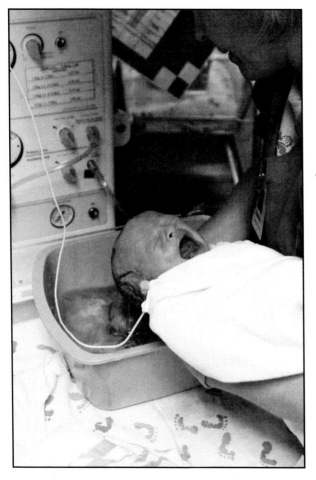

Write some first
impressions on
life from the
perspective of
this newborn.

How do you think God views time?

Purchase a set of finger paints and create an original work of art. As soon as you're finished, set aside 15 minutes to write about the experience.

Compose a poem that describes what this artist is feeling as she begins covering her canvas with paint.

Is this picture positive or negative? Why?

God perfectly formed each one of us, down to the smallest detail. Spend 10 minutes writing, thanking God for making you the way you are.

Write a dialogue between these two chess players.

Call to mind a piece of art that had an impact on you the first time you saw it. What was it about the piece that moved you?

Write the lyrics
to the song this
man is playing.

Come up with a title and a description
for this artist's creation.

Write a story explaining how these two
figures ended up in this field at sunset.

Write a battle
scene that
ends in the
destruction of
this tower.

Find someone who is willing to be your live model and have that person sit either outside or near a window on a sunny day. Arrange your model in a way where parts of his or her face are shadowed and parts are illuminated. Spend 10 minutes writing about your model's face, paying close attention to where the light falls.

Use this
picture as your
inspiration
for a poem.

Write down
what this man is
thinking about.

How does nature reflect the beauty of its Creator?

Gather together a blank sheet of paper, a small paintbrush, and watercolor paints. Use different colors of the paint to cover the entire sheet of paper with words describing who you were before you gave your life to Jesus. Once you are finished, take your sheet of paper outside and pour water on it until the colors blend together. Keep this small piece of art to remind you that your sins have been washed away and you are a colorful, beautiful, new creation in Christ.

Write about a time when following God
required you to journey alone for awhile.

Ongoing Prompts

Writing is a journey of discovery. It often takes more than an hour, more than a day, to uncover each piece of revelation and inspiration that a writing prompt may cause you to stumble upon.

This section of the book is filled with ongoing writing prompts that will require a longer period of time to complete. Even though the rest of the book is filled with prompts that can be responded to relatively quickly, I encourage you to take your time with those as well. Ponder your answer before you set pen to page. Respond to a prompt and then go back to the same prompt a year later, noting where your answers remain the same and where they differ.

One of my most treasured activities is reading through my old journals. Opening the cover of each well-worn journal instantly draws me back in time to where I was when I first penned the words on each page. The doodles I always seem to fit in around the words add just enough whimsy to elicit a smile. The words themselves remind me that I'm on a journey through the unknown to a heavenly home that becomes a little more familiar with each passing year.

It is encouraging to note the character development and maturity in my relationship with God that has taken place since the time I first started writing. My faith is stirred as I read through journal entries filled with prayers now answered. There's a simple beauty in a journal with pages that have only ever been traversed by one set of eyes. Sometimes it's best to write for an audience of one.

For the following prompts, I recommend writing your responses in a journal. This way, you'll have an organized, dated record of your writing. If you feel compelled to continue any of these prompts longer than the suggested times, indulge your inner writer. Use these exercises as an ongoing conversation with God.

Write a journal entry every day for a week. Have "faith" be the central theme of the journal entry each day. Ask God to strengthen your faith throughout the week.

Pick one of the following topics: love, joy, grace, suffering, or perseverance. Pray every day asking God for wisdom and revelation about that specific subject. Write a journal entry on that topic every day for two weeks. Let God continuously reveal more to you about the topic you chose.

This writing exercise will take four days. On the first day, write about your relationship with God the Father. The next day, write about your relationship with Jesus. On the third day, write about your relationship with the Holy Spirit. On the fourth day, answer the following questions: Which identity of the Triune God do you relate to the most? Which the least? Why do you think this is the case?

Make a commitment to write down every single dream you have for an entire month. It is crucial that you write the dream down immediately after waking from it (even if it's the middle of the night!), so have a pen and paper ready beside your bed. After the month is over, read through all of your dreams and select one to use as the foundation for a short story.

For one week, write out all of your prayers in a journal. Leave ample blank space at the end of each entry. Come back to these prayers a year from the date you wrote them down. In the space you left open under each prayer, write down any answers you've received to that prayer. Focus on being as specific as possible, both with your prayer requests and with your answers.

Commit to reading one psalm a day in the morning. Throughout the day, mediate on that particular psalm. At night, write a reaction to the psalm in your journal. Be sure to note specific verses that were relevant to your day.

For three days in a row, respond to this question: "Why are you alive?"

Write about something you've lost. Later on in the same day, write about something you've found.

Choose a favorite worship album. As soon as you wake up each morning, listen to one track from the album and then spend 15 minutes writing. Do this each morning until you've listened to all of the tracks on the album.

Commit to writing down your prayers for each member of your family. Write about one person each day.

Spend a week reading a chapter a day out of the Book of Proverbs. After you've finished each chapter, write about a verse that stood out to you that day.

No Limitations

When writing, it's all too easy to set parameters for yourself that limit creativity. To help curb this tendency, I came up with a special prompt for our weekly writers group. It was an exciting gathering, as we were meeting at the lake that night to write on a pontoon under the fading colors of an early fall evening. The assignment was for everyone to write for 20 minutes, with the one stipulation being that all of the writers include the word "tubuzwee" (a word I made up on the spot) somewhere in their poem or prose piece.

Although the prompt initially garnered a few questions, each writer quickly settled into crafting a scene where "tubuzwee" could effortlessly fit into. As the finished pieces were read, it turned out "tubuzwee" was a tree, a nonsense word, a tiny town, an ancient liquid, and a state of being. I was astonished at the originality of the work that resulted from this simple writing prompt. To date, the "tubuzwee" exercise has produced some of the most creative work that's come out of our weekly writers group.

Using a word that had no preexisting associations encouraged each writer to approach the exercise with an open mind. There was no right answer and no wrong answer. It was simply an opportunity to think creatively and free the imagination.

These prompts are designed to get you thinking in a new direction. Open your mind up to the possibilities these prompts present. Follow quickly after your initial reactions to get them down on paper, and save any refining for later.

If you had $1 million at your disposal to give away, what would you do with the money?

What color best describes your life?
Why?

If you were the architect in charge of designing your local church building, what would it look like?

If finances were not an issue whatsoever, how would that change your tomorrow?

Write about a person you know who best embodies the paradoxical term "dreaming awake."

Notice that in the word "revolution," the primary element is "revolve." Think of a revolution as the turning (revolving) of people's hearts. Write about what a revolution might look like in your community.

What life lesson, above all others, do you wish you would have learned at a younger age?

If you started up a new business, what would it be?

How many times today have you thought about tomorrow? How does your response to this question make you feel?

Write about a time when you were
surprised by your own boldness.

If you could live in any country other than your own, which would you pick and why?

What does true revival look like?

If you could build any building, what would it look like and what would its function be?

Who has God created you to be?

What more could you give to invest in
the lives of the people around you?

Compose a poem describing what it might
look like when a lion lies down with a lamb.
Use as many sensory details as you can.

Write about the best example you've ever witnessed of a group of people living in true Christian community. What do you think makes that specific community so successful?

How would your life be different if you were never influenced by the fear of man?

Write about the future you feel God has for a friend of yours. Now, write about how you could help that person live out his or her calling. Include practical ways as well as spiritual support.

How much does a memory weigh?

Write about a business person who you see as a good example of a "missionary in the marketplace."

Make a list of five statements you used to think were true, but have since discovered to be false.

If you could spend one month of your life either working in an orphanage or helping to build a church, which would you choose and why?

What is the best gift you've ever given?

What hinders you from boldly declaring the Gospel of Jesus to the people around you who need to hear this life-saving message?

Begin a piece of writing (prose or a poem) with the line: "Wake up, dreamers!"

Come up with a top 10 list titled "How to Slow the World Down."

What miracle do you most desire to witness?

When did you find your voice?

Write for 10 minutes using "In my dreams I am able to …" as the beginning of your writing entry.

What is God seeing as He looks at the earth right now?

God's Words

"While working to clean out some abandoned apartments in Chicago's Cabrini Green neighborhood, a bunch of women from a local church came together and made us lunch. The poverty these people lived in completely astounded me as a young teenager. I had no idea people in our nation were living in such squalor.

"I scooped up shovelful after shovelful of rotten food, clothing, baby toys, and syringes from living room floors. For a moment, my reality melded with the reality of the lives of the people who once occupied the abandoned apartments my youth group was cleaning.

"It was the lunch that impacted me the most. The ladies who cooked for us had nothing, literally nothing—in a way I couldn't possibly understand. Yet, they wanted to give us something. They set before me a pile of cold, dry, sticky noodles with a sprinkling of shredded cheese on top as the only flavor.

"I remember feeling more grateful for that meal, for that moment, than anything I had ever experienced before in my 16 years. Although I've since been blessed with the opportunity to sample some of the world's best dishes, that meal is the one I know I'll never forget.

"Cold noodles. Shredded cheese. The meal that changed me."

This account comes out of my journal as a response to a prompt asking for something simple or seemingly insignificant that impacted me in a major way. When I first heard that prompt, I immediately knew I should write about my journey to Chicago as a part of a short-term missions trip with my church.

Years after my youth group's week in Chicago, I still remember the taste of that meal. Even though I can no longer recall most of the details of our trip, that one moment is fixed in my mind as vividly as if I was currently sitting in that cold church basement getting ready to lift my plastic fork and partake of the unusual meal set before me. The hospitable women who served me those noodles and cheese remind me of the widow who Jesus commended for her generous offering.

> *"As Jesus looked up, he saw the rich putting their gifts into the temple treasury. He also saw a poor widow put in two very small copper coins. 'Truly I tell you,' he said, 'this poor widow has put in more than all the others. All these people gave their gifts out of their wealth; but she out of her poverty put in all she had to live on.'"* (LUKE 21:1-4, NIV)

The following exercises are each connected to the Bible. Meditate on the passages mentioned and take your time when responding. The Living Word of God is filled with endless writing-related possibilities.

A preacher once said, "We need to move from being the woman at the well to Jesus at the well." Read the account of Jesus encountering the Samaritan woman at the well (*JOHN 4:1-42*). What does this preacher's statement mean to you?

Rewrite the story of the woman at the well, set in modern times. Instead of having Jesus encounter a woman at a well, have the meeting take place at a coffee shop. Pay close attention to the dialogue, making sure it resonates with what a woman would say today.

Read Luke 8:40-48, where Jesus heals a woman who touches the edge of His garment. What does this account reveal about the healing power of Christ?

Who is your favorite person in the Bible?
Why?

Write a journal entry from Mary's perspective the night after her son was crucified on the cross.

Colossians 1:24-27 references *"the mystery that has been kept hidden for ages and generations, but is now disclosed to the saints."* God freely chooses to reveal His purposes to His children, and gives us the wisdom and revelation necessary to comprehend these mysteries. What is the most recent mystery God has unveiled to you?

What is your favorite Bible verse? Write about a time when this verse seemed most relevant to your life.

While Noah heeded God and built the ark, those around him mocked his every effort. Write about an "ark building" experience either in your life or the life of a friend. Did the mockers change their tone when the "flood" came and God's plan was revealed?

Write a poem from the perspective of an eyewitness at the crucifixion. Include sensory language from all five senses (sight, hearing, touch, smell, and taste).

What can a person learn about true leadership from examining the accounts of Jesus revealed in the Gospel of John?

"But store up for yourselves treasures in heaven, where moths and vermin do not destroy, and where thieves do not break in and steal. For where your treasure is, there your heart will be also." (MATTHEW 6:20-21, NIV)

What treasure have you stored up in heaven?

Who is your least favorite person in the Bible?
Why?

Read the account of Samson in Judges 16. Verse 20 reveals how Samson forfeited the calling of God on his life without even knowing it. In Samson's case, he gave up his strength for a woman. Is there anything in your life that you are putting before the destiny God has for you?

Take a verse from the Song of Solomon and
use it as the last line in a love poem.

Read Acts 2 and pay close attention to the characteristics of the early church. Compare this with the common characteristics of the church today.

"Those who cling to their worthless idols forfeit the grace that could be theirs." (JONAH 2:8, NIV) Jonah made this statement while praying to God from inside the belly of a fish. Write about a revelation you've had that's come out of a difficult life situation.

End Notes

Inciting an enthusiasm for writing in others and teaching on writing as a form of worship are two of my favorite pursuits. As the facilitator of two ongoing writers groups, I've learned the importance of encouraging creativity in emerging writers while still working to challenge those who are more advanced in the craft.

There is a place for writing in everyone's life. More often than not, I've found people just need a little assistance in either getting started or in exploring new avenues with their writing. Whether you'd like to grow as an individual writer, or have an interest in starting a writers group in your area, consider hosting a writing workshop to benefit the writers in your community.

The writing workshops I offer range in length from just an hour or two to an intensive writing course. Writers of all ages and abilities leave these workshops with a renewed passion for writing and a desire to impact the world with words.

Artistic collaboration workshops are also offered. In these sessions, writing is introduced along with other creative outlets such as music, visual art, and dance. Different genres of artists combine their God-given talents to inspire participants to do the same. Witnessing and participating in these live, multi-genre arts workshops revolutionizes and invigorates the creative process in those attending.

If your community, church, or local writers group is interested in hosting a writing workshop, visit www.heidikratzke.com and contact me from there.

About the Author

Heidi Kratzke is a writer and visual artist who is passionate about inspiring, encouraging, and challenging fellow artists. She is a graduate of Minnesota State University Moorhead, with a degree in English-Creative Writing Emphasis. She has worked as a writer and photographer for several newspapers, in addition to pursuing freelance writing.

Along with her husband, Jonathan, Heidi is owner of Creative Culture Media—a website, graphic design, and writing business. She serves on the board of directors for the Lake Region Writers Network, facilitates writing workshops, and has started two regional writers groups. Her writing has been published in magazines, newspapers, and literary journals.

Heidi and Jonathan currently reside in Ottertail, Minn., in a beautiful old house they share with their generally loving and always ravenous cat, Little Tuna.